GARDENING WITHOUT SOIL

BOOKSALE

GARDENING WITHOUT SOIL

SARAH R. RIEDMAN

ILLUSTRATED BY
ROD SLATER

FRANKLIN WATTS
NEW YORK | LONDON | 1979
A FIRST BOOK

ACKNOWLEDGMENTS

The author is most grateful to Dr. Ronald F. Howells and his Special Resource Class at the Jensen
Beach Elementary School for the privilege of observing their labors and fun during a successful
project—growing tomatoes without soil, and to Dr.
Howells for his help in other ways, including his
critical reading of the manuscript; and to Mr. Paul
Y. Chamberlain for his generosity during several
extended visits to Love Apple Acres in Stuart, and
for clarifying the many operations of a commercial
hydroponic unit.

Library of Congress Cataloging in Publication Data

Riedman, Sarah Regal, 1902–
    Gardening without soil.

    (A First book)
    Bibliography: p.
    Includes index.
    SUMMARY: An introduction to hydroponics,
what it is, how it is done, why it is useful, and its
potential for future use, with directions for setting
up your own project.
    1. Hydroponics—Juvenile literature. [1. Hy-
droponics. 2. Gardening] I. Title
SB126.5.R53   635'.04'8   78–13088
ISBN 0–531–02256–0

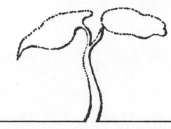

CONTENTS

GARDENING
WITHOUT SOIL

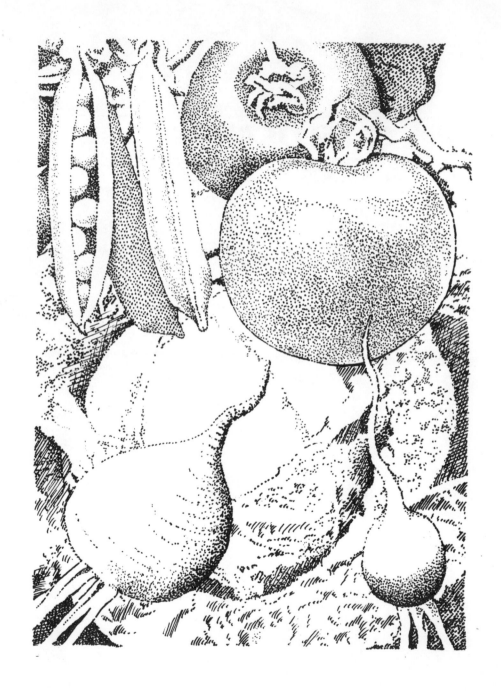

GARDENS WITHOUT SOIL

In 1929 Dr. William F. Gericke, professor of botany at the University of California, harvested 1,226 pounds (557 kg) of tomatoes on a hundredth of an acre (0.004 hectare) of growing surface *without soil or manure*. He grew his plants with only water and chemicals. His soilless-cultured tomato plants reached a height of 25 feet (7.62 m). He had to pick his crop from a ladder. The professor coined the name HYDRO-PONICS for the method of growing plants without soil. The term is derived from two Greek words: *hudor* meaning "water" and *ponos*, "work."

BACK TO BEGINNINGS

The name hydroponics is new, but the method had been tried for some time. When and where did it all start? Some people trace its roots to nearly three centuries ago. Dr. John Woodward, an English physician and a Fellow of the Royal Society of England, wondered what raw materials plants need to make their food. What nourished crops—the water or the solid particles in soil? So he grew plants in polluted water. In 1697 he reported to the Society that the solid particles in the soil did indeed contribute to plant growth.

Advances in chemical knowledge made possible the discovery of the many chemicals in soil. This led to the development of ways to furnish plants with chemicals required for growth, without using soil. Jean Baptiste Boussingault, a French scientist who began as a mineralogist employed by a mining company, turned to agricultural chemistry. In the early 1850s he grew plants in pots filled with charcoal and sand to which he added water and chemicals of known composition.

A decade later Julius von Sachs, professor of botany at the University of Würzburg, Germany, added balanced proportions of fertilizer chemicals to water. Under controlled conditions he grew plants in soilless cultures. Scientists in other countries carried out such experiments for the next half century. They aimed to find the most suitable concentrations of nutrient elements for satisfactory plant growth.

Dr. Gericke's success story of a crop grown solely on water and a nutrient formula took the solution-culture method out of the laboratory and into practical horticulture. News about hydroponics spread quickly and widely. Many people became interested in soilless culture as a hobby. Some small commercial ventures were also started, particularly in California and Florida, where the climate permits year-round outdoor growth.

The first use of hydroponics on a large scale came during World War II. The armed forces of the United States set up hydroponic units at military bases on the barren islands of the Pacific. In wartime the shipping of fresh vegetables to overseas outposts was not practical, and a coral island is not a place to grow them. Hydroponics solved the problem.

HYDROPONICS TODAY

Today hydroponic gardens both out-of-doors and in greenhouses flourish somewhere on every continent. They are found in the Sahara Desert, the Arabian peninsula, Kuwait, Lebanon, Israel (particularly in the Negev Desert and along the Dead Sea), India, Malaysia, the Seychelles, the Canary Islands, the Bahamas, and Puerto Rico. Soilless culture is practiced not only in sandy wastes, but also in Western European countries, Australia, New Zealand, the Soviet Union, Mexico, Brazil, Hawaii, and Alaska.

Hydroponics as a way of practical crop cultivation is used throughout the world. Continued research is coordinated by the International Working-Group on Soilless Culture. Through this organization hydroponicists all over the world exchange experiences, consult, and advise new participants in crop growing by this method.

In the United States and Canada hundreds of commercial operations grow crops for market, especially near large population centers. Units have also been set up in small towns and suburbs. And anyone can grow favorite vegetables in a bucket or a window box, on the roof of an apartment building or in a backyard, at home or in the school yard. It is not impossible

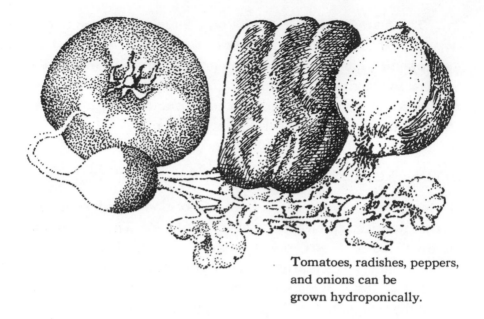

Tomatoes, radishes, peppers,
and onions can be
grown hydroponically.

that astronauts may grow hydroponic crops in the space
shuttle or colony of the future.

SOILLESS CULTURE
VERSUS DIRT FARMING

Why not grow plants in soil as they have been grown throughout the centuries? Or why, if crops can be grown hydroponically, do we need soil at all? The answer is that hydroponics
is more expensive than soil cultivation if water and fertile soil
are available. Hydroponics is suitable where the soil is infertile, diseased, or poisoned and water scarce. Hydroponic
units readily fit into limited space in towns and cities, where
land is scarce and too valuable for growing crops.

Where space is a problem, soilless culture has the distinct advantage of providing a crop many times larger than a crop grown in soil on an equal size area of land. For example, in one hydroponic operation, the yield of tomatoes per acre (.4 hectare) was eighteen times greater than it would have been using the conventional soil method.

Where rainfall is scanty and irrigation not feasible or too costly, hydroponics is also advantageous. The water is recycled, so that as much as or more than 90 percent of the water needed to grow field crops is saved. The amount varies with the degree of evaporation, depending on time of day, season, or location, for example the desert. When grown in closed units under controlled conditions crops can be grown year-round without concern about drought, wind, snow, soil diseases, or pests. Rarely do pesticides have to be used.

GROW HYDROPONICALLY

Tomatoes and watermelons, cabbage and bell peppers, radishes and onions, and lots more have been grown by soilless culture. But it would be wrong to assume that success is assured without tending. As in soil, plants raised without soil must get proper care. Hydroponics is both an art and a science. For a flourishing hydroponic garden you will need to learn all the steps in setting it up and in operating it, as well as knowing why each step is important. Problems will arise, and things may go wrong. The hydroponic gardener has to be prepared to recognize the problems, avoid pitfalls, and to correct what goes wrong.

THE HYDROPONIC SYSTEM
Part I: Container and Soil Substitute

All living organisms need food to grow and reproduce. Plants *make* their food but have to be furnished with the raw materials to build their tissues and to grow and form seeds for more plants. They need light, air, water, mineral salts, and support for the roots. Green plants require sunlight or artificial light and carbon dioxide, which they get from the air. The soil supplies water, mineral salts, and anchors the plant.

In a hydroponic garden we provide for two essentials of plant growth furnished by soil: a balanced nutrient solution to feed the plant and physical support to keep it in an erect position directed toward the light. The nutrient solution, or formula, consisting of chemically known minerals in proper proportions, is much the same for all hydroponic systems. However, the method used to support the plants depends on the choice of the hydroponic unit.

CHOICE OF HYDROPONIC UNIT

Do you want to grow your garden indoors, in an outdoor window box, on a roof, an open porch, a patio, or in a yard? How large will your garden be? If indoors, will there be adequate light for your plants? Too much light, from either eastern or western exposure when the sun is beating down on hot days, would be injurious. Northern exposure on cold or dull days may not provide enough light.

If the plan is for a garden of ambitious size, you will need to consider the space, its relationship to the light source, and nearness to the water supply. Do you live in an area where the climate will permit all-year growth or where the crop will have to be seasonal?

Next you will have to consider what you will grow your plants in.

Regardless of the size of your projected garden, however simple or sophisticated, a hydroponic unit involves these basic elements: 1) the *container,* 2) the *aggregate* (soil substitute) or a way to keep the plant erect without aggregate, and 3) a *water supply.*

THE CONTAINER

The variety of vessels that can serve as containers is almost limitless. Here is a sampling of containers that have been used: flower pot, bucket, window box, earthenware crock, dishpan, large jar, cat-litter pan, and an old kitchen sink. All containers must be of leak-proof material, made of plastic, stoneware, or glass but *not* metal. It must have a hole to permit

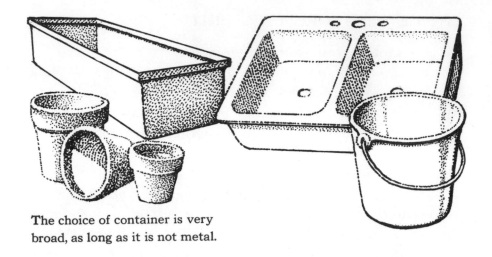

The choice of container is very broad, as long as it is not metal.

drainage, with a stopper to fit when the solution is not being drained. A flower pot and an old kitchen sink already have a hole. In the other containers a hole may be made with a drill. Plastic tubs or trays used for window boxes have holes or have marks in the base where holes can be punched out. Also, pots for hanging plants have holes along with an attached pan into which the solution will drain.

In the early days of soilless culture, plants were grown *suspended* in nutrient solution. If you choose to use a large beaker or wide glass jar as a container, make a hole in the lid, large enough to lower the roots into the solution. To keep the rest of the plant above the lid, narrow down the opening with modeling clay or some other material making a collar around the hole. In this arrangement the plant is suspended rather than supported as it would be in soil—or in aggregate—to be described later.

This was actually the way Dr. Gericke grew his plants—

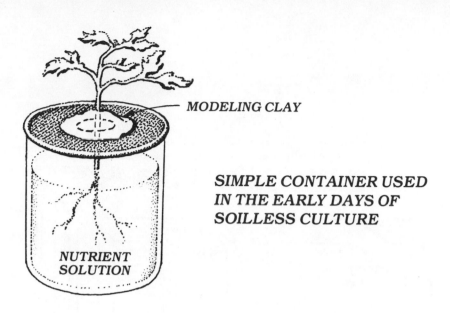

MODELING CLAY

SIMPLE CONTAINER USED
IN THE EARLY DAYS OF
SOILLESS CULTURE

NUTRIENT
SOLUTION

in shallow tanks containing the nutrients. The top of each tank was covered by a platform built over the tank. The cover kept the light away from the roots to prevent growth of algae (microscopic green plants). The platform, also called the "litter bearer," was used to prop up the plants.

THE "LITTER BEARER"

A rectangular wooden frame on four legs was set up so that it sat over the tank, leaving an air space of several inches between tank and frame. Wide-mesh wire was stretched across the frame and covered with about 3 inches (7.6 cm) of wood shavings. The plants were set so that the roots passed through the mesh holes into the solution and were kept in place by the wood shavings. Another way to stabilize the plants is to place a sheet of styrofoam over the tank, with holes for inserting the plants.

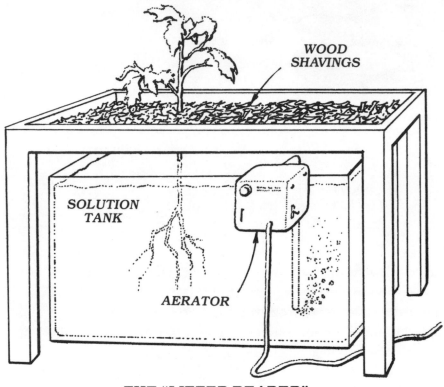

WOOD
SHAVINGS

SOLUTION
TANK

AERATOR

THE "LITTER BEARER"

You might think that roots immersed in solution would grow fast by taking up lots of nutrient. But this isn't so because the method does not provide for aeration. Without air reaching the roots they would soon die. To solve this problem, air may be pumped in by an electric aerator similar to that used in a fish aquarium.

Today, water culture, as this method is called, is rarely used, and is replaced by aggregate culture.

CONSTRUCTING
A LARGE UNIT

If there is room for a large hydroponic unit, the container could be a series of fiberglass beds available commercially and custom built to fit the space. Or anyone handy could build one or more vats, also called troughs, benches, or beds. They can be made of concrete, wood, or plastic. Common dimensions are 20 feet (6.1 m) long, 2 feet (0.6 m) wide, and about 8 inches (20 cm) deep. If concrete is the material used, a wood frame is constructed, and the concrete is set from Sakrete, in ready-mixed proportions of cement and sand. Or it can be made from concrete blocks used in setting building foundations. If the beds are made of wood, they should be raised from the ground to avoid rotting and the introduction of soil organisms. Also, for greater convenience in care, beds could be set up on platforms about 2 feet (0.6 m) from the ground. This proved to be a good arrangement for a hydroponic project in an enclosed, roofless area of a school playground.

Concrete vats are painted with high-grade asphalt paint to prevent corrosion and toxicity to the plants. Even some kinds of wood may be toxic. Instead of asphalt paint the same purpose is served by lining wood containers with black, heavy-duty polyethylene plastic sheeting. The plastic should be drawn over the edges of the bed and nailed down.

One end of the bed is raised by placing a 1-inch (2.5-cm) plank under it. This tilts it sufficiently to provide gravity flow for draining the solution after feeding. In one outdoor operation, the floor was built to slope toward the center forming a V-shaped bottom along the full length of the vat. Half-tiles cut from earthenware pipes about 4 inches (10 cm) in diameter were placed over the midline in the floor. This arrangement formed a pipe for gravity flow through a single drain at one end.

In the school project, two openings were bored at the lower end of the vat. Each hole was fitted with heavy plastic tubing for drainage, and they were closed with caps, removed only for draining. (Metal plumbing is avoided because it interacts with the nutrients.)

THE AGGREGATE

Once the container is selected and built to the specification of the grower, an inert soil substitute—the *aggregate*—is put in place. Its sole purpose is to support the plant, substituting for the anchorage function of soil. There are almost as many choices of aggregate types as containers. Whatever material is selected as the growing medium must have the following features: 1) be porous to permit aeration of the roots; 2) hold water and nutrients; 3) not be toxic to the plants; and 4) not interact with the nutrient solution.

Among aggregates used are wheat straw bales, wood chips and shavings, sawdust, redwood bark, pine bark, crushed brick, peat moss, cinders mixed with sand, rock wool—an insulating material used in Scandinavian countries—plastic chips, two so-called "man-made" substances—perlite (a volcanic rock) and vermiculite (related to mica rock)—and gravel, the most common.

How do you choose an aggregate? Every hydroponic grower has a preference for one or another, but availability

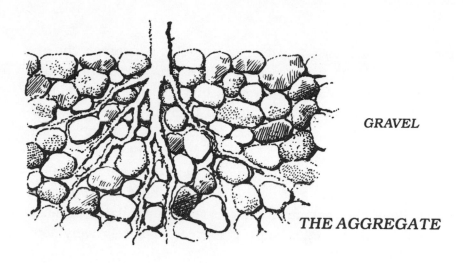

GRAVEL

THE AGGREGATE

and cost are important, after considering the properties of each kind of aggregate. For example, straw generates heat up to a temperature of 180° F (82.5° C), which kills microorganisms, making it a sterile medium. On the other hand, when wet, straw rots, inviting fungus growth and mildews. Wood shavings, sawdust, and cinders where available are cheap, if not free. But sawdust may hold too much water, and cinders are often acid and would have to be soaked in sodium hydroxide to be neutralized. Perlite crystals reflect light and may actually scorch the plant.

Vermiculite splits like mica or cleaves into clean, thin layers that curl like a worm, from which it gets its name. When heated to a temperature of 2,000° F (1,093° C), it expands many times. As a result it is light in weight and readily absorbs water and air—features most desired in a growing medium. Its chief advantage as an aggregate is that it is sterile, but because it requires factory pretreatment it is more costly than other aggregates. And some growers find it retains too much water.

Because it is easy to get, river gravel is a common choice. Gravel is a loose mixture of pebbles and rock fragments coarser than sand. Gravel comes in bits the size of a grain of rice to pebbles of about half an inch (1.25 cm). The preferred size is three-eighths of an inch (0.93 cm), known as pea gravel. The many-faceted shape of the pebbles lends high porosity, good aeration, and less retention of water. Gravel is free of toxic material and does not absorb heat or favor mildew. It holds the roots firmly and is readily available in most places from construction supply sources at a relatively low cost.

It would be nice if gravel came sterile from the supply source, but it doesn't. The next best thing is to wash it—hose or brush-scrub it—to remove soil particles that harbor bacteria and sometimes *nematodes* (tiny worms). These soil inhabitants can damage the roots. In a hydroponic garden we have to start with aggregate free of disease producers.

THE HYDROPONIC SYSTEM
Part II: Water Supply

For a home or school hydroponic unit, the household water source is perfectly suitable. The water you drink will also support the growth of your plants. A hose hooked into an outdoor water outlet or faucet will deliver fresh water. For a large operation it may be more convenient to furnish water from another source, such as a well. This does not mean that a large supply is required, since in a hydroponic system the water is recycled. This is one of the important advantages of hydroponics. As little as 3 percent of the water required by plants in soil is used in a soilless garden.

To determine the suitability of the water from the special source it is analyzed by a commercial chemical laboratory. (For the grower who has any doubt about the water supply, the local water supply company, city water department, or the country agricultural agent will advise concerning the "hardness" or "softness," or any other relevant characteristic.)

An analysis would indicate, in parts per million (ppm) the quantity of each mineral constituent, the amount of chlorine in the water, its acid-alkaline balance, whether the water is "hard" and, among other things, its color, odor, turbidity, and bacterial count.

Of the minerals, those that contribute to "hardness" are calcium and magnesium salts. If there is a really excessive amount of these salts, they will accumulate in the plumbing connections and even on the roots. It would then be necessary to adjust for these minerals in the nutrient solution. But moderately hard water would not affect the growth of your plants. Excessive chlorine is injurious but chlorine-treated water is not likely to have too high a concentration for plants.

ACID-ALKALINE BALANCE

The acid-alkaline balance of water is especially important for hydroponic culture; it definitely affects plant growth. This balance is expressed by the symbol pH (H stands for hydrogen ion [H+]). Pure water is neither acid nor alkaline, having a pH of 7.0, or neutral. A pH below 7.0 signifies acid; above 7.0 alkaline. The pH range for satisfactory growth of most vegetables is between pH 6.0 and 7.0.

In the care of your plants you will have to check the pH of the nutrient solution twice a week and to adjust it if it is out of range. You will find out how to test the pH and to adjust it for best growth later.

What about using salt water? According to a British authority on soilless culture, it was once thought that a salt content of 2,500 parts per million would be too salty for gar-

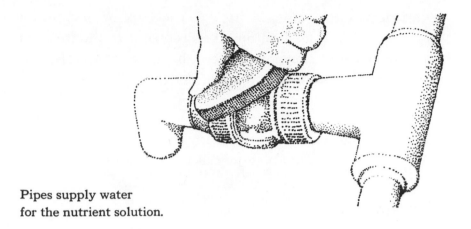

Pipes supply water
for the nutrient solution.

dens. However, recent research work in North Africa showed that plants will tolerate very saline water, even seawater, as long as there is *good drainage and free movement through the growing medium.*

On the other hand, rainwater, which we are likely to think of as close to "pure" water, contains dissolved nitrogen, oxygen, and carbon dioxide, as well as certain harmful impurities, especially near large industrial centers. Excessive amounts of carbon dioxide would render the water slightly acid, but probably not below pH 6.5.

PLUMBING CONNECTIONS

The water is supplied through pipes from the source to the tank for storing the nutrient solution. Through other pipes the nutrient solution is supplied to the growing medium in the vats. Depending upon the particular unit, other pipes drain the nutrients either directly back to the tank or first into a vessel to catch the solution and then return it to the tank. In more complicated units, in which the nutrient solution is pumped in, the same pipe both delivers and drains the solution.

The pipes, the tank, and other vessels should be plastic. Metals, especially iron, interact with the minerals in the nutrient solution and could be injurious to the plants.

FLOODING AND DRAINING ARRANGEMENTS

Let's start with the gravel aggregate in the container filled to about 2 inches (5 cm) from the top. How do you flood the tray, vat, or bed? And how much nutrient solution will be needed? Usually a 30- to 60-gallon (136- to 272-liter) tank is adequate for the amount of solution required for a large garden. Where a pump is used to flood the aggregate, the tank is usually placed underground, below the beds. Whatever size container is used, the tank should hold twice the amount of solution required to fill the bed. Actually, you do not fill it to the top. It is important that the top inch (2.5 cm) of aggregate be dry. Flooding to the top will cause growth of algae. Even when only moist, the gravel may become mildewed.

Let's assume that you decided to have your garden indoors and that your container was a plastic tub and the "tank" a plastic pail. You would need a hole (an inch—2.5 cm—or less) at the bottom of the pail, and one (same size) in the side of the tub. You would connect the tub and tank by a length of plastic hose. If you set the pail on a high stool or a shelf above

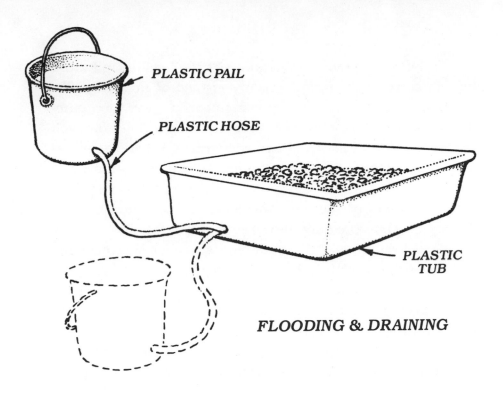

PLASTIC PAIL

PLASTIC HOSE

PLASTIC TUB

FLOODING & DRAINING

the growing tray, the flooding will take place by gravity. As soon as the tub is flooded, the pail is set on the floor, below the growing tray stand, for draining. In this way gravity flow is achieved through the same tube in both directions. You simply raise and lower the pail containing the nutrient solution.

The draining is as important as the feeding, so that the roots are submerged in a nonaerated condition for only a brief time. Remember that as the solution drains off, air replaces it in the aggregate's spaces. The flooding and draining process is done twice a day.

In larger and more elaborate units the feeding and draining are accomplished mechanically instead of manually. The solution is pumped into the growing beds or trays by a pump inside the tank. The pumping is regulated by a timer for cyclical feeding and draining, again twice a day. When the pumping is completed—a matter of 8 or 10 minutes—the pump automatically shuts off. Since the tank is about 2 feet (0.6 m) below the level of the vats, the solution is drained back by gravity flow into the tank for reuse. The timer has been set for the next flooding, and the pumping will start automatically. Whatever the mechanical device, the principle is clearly the same as in a nonautomated, manual unit. The solution is recycled even if you drain off the solution by hand into buckets so it is returned to the vats. This is called a *closed system*.

A garden in a bucket could also yield a crop by what is known as an *open system*. If you need any convincing that plants will grow without soil, try the open bucket method, and you need not bother with hose connections. All you need is a plastic, 5-gallon (20-liter) bucket. Drill five or six holes in the bottom, and fill the bucket with aggregate. In such small quantities it would not be too costly to use vermiculite. Fill the bucket to within 3 inches (7.5 cm) of the top. You can get the dry nutrients in the same store with instructions for preparing the solution. And you are ready to start your plants.

In this—the open system—you feed twice a day, but you don't recover the solution. It will drain out into the ground and fertilize the lawn. This would, of course, be wasteful in a large hydroponic unit, but it is an easy way to get a start in soilless gardening.

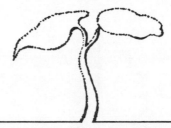

STARTING
THE PLANTS

The plants in your hydroponic system can be started either from seeds or from seedlings. The seeds you buy from a garden center or a seed company are dry and, therefore, dormant. Seeds will not develop into plants unless they are given a favorable environment. A seedling is a young plant started in soil. When about 6 inches (15 cm) high it is ready to be placed into a hydroponic unit. Usually seedlings are bought from nurseries, where the seeds were planted in flats, small boxes containing potting soil. You can, of course, start your plants from seeds yourself.

A seed is a plant embryo contained in a natural packet of stored food—oil and starch. Under the right conditions of temperature and moisture the seed will *germinate* or sprout. This happens after seeds are buried in a pot of soil and watered, or placed in moist sawdust, or even put between a couple of thicknesses of wet towel paper. For most hydroponic

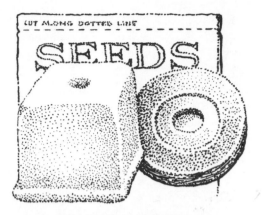

STARTING WITH SEEDS

SEEDLING

systems the plants are started by the "one-step" method, using a variety of seed-starting containers. Different ones come by the names Jiffy Pellets, GRO-blocks, and Peat Pots. They are made of compressed peat or seaweed, to which a little fertilizer has been added. These seed-starting containers vary in shape: little cubes about an inch-and-a-half (about 4 cm), the same size cubes but narrowed at the top, or circular rolls depressed in the middle. All have a little hole at the top.

You sow two seeds in each of these blocks, water lightly, and place the blocks on a tray inside a large clear plastic or cellophane bag, tied off at the open end. When finished it looks like a rectangular transparent balloon with the tray inside. The plants will be ready to go into the hydroponic unit when they are about 3 inches (7.5 cm) high. They are placed in the aggregate without removing them from the starting containers. After a while the roots will break through the seed-starting containers and into the aggregate.

If you start with seedlings, they should be gently lifted out of the soil, taking care not to injure the roots. The roots should be carefully washed free of all soil—an added precaution of not introducing soil organisms into a soilless garden. Then they are ready to be placed in the aggregate, at a depth of about 2 inches (5 cm).

FROM SEED TO SEEDLING

Under the conditions described and roughly at room temperatures—about 75° F (24° C)—the seed germinates. The seed absorbs enough water so that the outer skin bursts, and the tiny embryo starts to develop. The greater part of the seed consists of two "seed leaves," or *cotyledons*, where most of the reserve food is stored. Between the cotyledons and attached to them is a short axis.

As sharply pointed part of the axis below the cotyledons, called the *hypocotyl*, is the young rootlet. It forces its way downward and eventually forms the primary root. The upper part of the axis, the *epicotyl*, grows upward toward the light and develops into the stem. Soon young, green leaves grow out on tendrils from the stem.

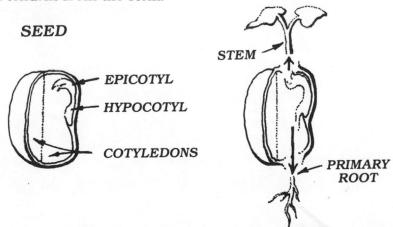

SEED

EPICOTYL

HYPOCOTYL

COTYLEDONS

STEM

PRIMARY ROOT

At this point in the development of the young plant, its reserve food is nearly exhausted, and it begins to make its own food. The stem continues to grow, branches out, and the plant leafs out broadly and grows taller. The leaves then manufacture food for all the tissues of the plant, including the root. Some of the food is stored in the root but most goes to provide the material for growth of ever more branches and leaves. Growth upward and downward proceeds simultaneously. With added leaf growth, the root growth and support increase. More branches reach out for raw materials.

In the hydroponic system, root growth is much less than in soil. There is not great expansion of the root system because the raw materials are regularly supplied as nutrient solution. Consequently there is no stimulus for root wandering for nutrients. The hydroponically grown plant gets enough raw materials from the solution to reach full size in height, leaf growth, and fruit development.

FOOD FOR
THE PLANTS

The nutrients furnished to plants have to be dissolved in water, just as they are dissolved in water in the soil. The nutrients are chemicals of two classes: major, or *macro*, elements and *micro*, *trace* or minor, elements. Early studies showed that the nutrient solution must contain five (or six) elements: nitrogen, phosphorus, potassium, calcium, and magnesium; in some formulas sulfur is also included as an essential element; in others as a trace element. These elements are supplied as salts: for example, nitrogen as potassium nitrate or as ammonium sulfate. The ammonium part of the salt contains the nitrogen. This is because nitrogen—a gas—cannot be used by the plant in that form. Similarly, the other minerals also come as salts, such as calcium nitrate and magnesium sulfate.

With later research it was found that plants, just as do animals and humans, require minute amounts of other ele-

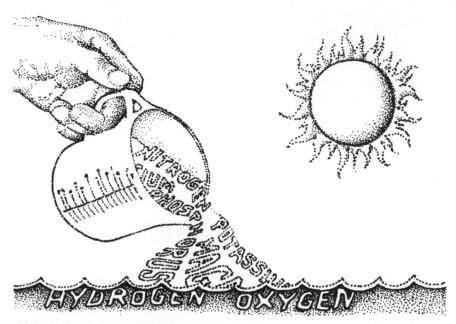

Chemicals provide the food to grow on.

ments: iron, manganese, boron, copper, zinc, molybdenum, chlorine, and the list is growing—iodine, cobalt? They are required in extremely small amounts, which is why they are called the micro or trace elements.

The other required elements are carbon, hydrogen, and oxygen: coming from carbon dioxide from air and hydrogen and oxygen (combined in water) from the soil and through the roots.

THE BALANCED FORMULA

The nutrients have to be present in certain definite proportions to make a balanced formula. For instance, the ratio of nitrogen to potassium must be at least equal or up to twice or three times the amount of potassium as nitrogen. On dark or short days (winter) the smaller proportion of nitrogen to potassium has been found by experience to work well. On bright days and at high temperatures greater amounts of nitrogen are needed.

The amount of each nutrient is commonly given in parts per million (ppm) of water. One gram of the mineral in 1,000 liters of water is one part per million (1 cubic centimeter of water weighs 1 gram). There are 1,000 cubic centimeters in 1 liter. A thousand liters are the same as 264 gallons.

Below is an example of a formula from the Agricultural Experiment Station of Purdue University. It gives the amount of each chemical (in grams) for preparing a balanced solution in the proportions needed of nitrogen, potassium, phosphorus, magnesium, and calcium in parts per million.

FORMULA FOR 1,000 LITERS (264 GALLONS)

MACRO NUTRIENTS	PPM	CHEMICAL	GRAMS*
Nitrogen	110	Calcium nitrate	710
Potassium	300	Potassium sulfate	750
Phosphorus	65	Monocalcium phosphate	308
Magnesium	50	Magnesium sulfate	537
Calcium	189	(The two calcium sources above provide)	

* 28.35 grams equal 1 oz.

Formulas differ according to the salts used to provide the essential elements, as is seen in the text formula, recommended by the U.S. Department of Agriculture.

CHEMICAL	QUANTITY IN OUNCES	GRAMS	MACRO NUTRIENTS SUPPLIED
Ammonium sulfate	1.5	43	Nitrogen, Sulfur
Potassium nitrate	9	255	Nitrogen, Potassium
Monocalcium phosphate	4	113	Phosphorus, Calcium
Magnesium sulfate	6	170	Magnesium, Sulfur
Calcium sulfate	7	198	Calcium, Sulfur

As you see in the last column, nitrogen could come from two different salts, sulfur from three, and calcium from two, but both of the formulas in the tables furnish the essential macro nutrients in the necessary proportions.

There are similar formulas for the trace elements. But since they are required in extremely small amounts, one would have to use a chemical scale or else weigh out quantities many times larger than needed for even a large garden. Besides, an enormous tank would be needed to dissolve them in. In many commercial fertilizers the trace elements are present as impurities in quantities sufficient for most purposes. (Iron in the form of iron sulfate is sometimes added without even weighing, just as a "pinch of salt" is added in cooking or baking recipes.)

Now that you see how the formulas are prepared, you

will be relieved to learn that you don't have to go through all that weighing and calculating. In fact, it may be difficult to obtain the individual salts in garden centers or retail drug stores. For most hydroponic operations, including commercial greenhouses, the nutrients are bought as prepared formulas in powder form and in the balanced proportions. The mixture is then dissolved in water, according to the amount stated on the label. It is easier than following a cook book recipe: just dissolve 1 teaspoon (5 ml) in a gallon (4 liters) of water! And you have a balanced nutrient solution—food for your plants.

Still, it is important to know what the formula contains, especially when, for one reason or other, plants do not thrive. To solve the problem you may need to adjust the formula. But most of the time you can count on the formula to be foolproof.

Nutrient mixtures are available in garden stores, from supply houses specializing in soluble fertilizers, or in stores, such as Sears, J. C. Penney, and others, that have a special plant department.

PLANT YOUR HYDROPONIC GARDEN

As soon as you have set up your hydroponic unit, the aggregate is in, the nutrient solution ready, and the seedlings about 6 inches (15 cm) high, you are ready to plant your garden. Gently remove each plant from the flat, taking care not to injure the roots. Rinse them free of soil, using a sprinkling can rather than a hose, so as not to break off any of the tender roots with the force of the stream. Then make a little pit in the gravel, about 1 inch (2.5 cm) deep, spreading the pebbles with your finger. Insert the seedling and gently firm up the roots by putting the pebbles back in place. Tomato plants should be set between 8 and 12 inches (20 to 30 cm) apart. Beans would not need to be that far apart. The spacing depends on the plants you choose for your garden. Scallions could be only 4 inches (10 cm) apart, while cabbage plants, which grow low but spread out horizontally, may require 1 foot (30 cm) or more for additional surface space. If more than one kind of plant is grown at the same time, it is desirable to alternate a low with a tall plant: one cabbage alternating with one tomato, for example, to permit access to light for each.

Make a pit in the gravel,
and place the seedling in it.

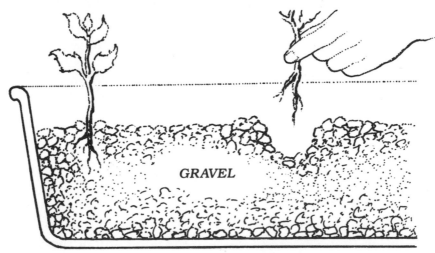

GRAVEL

CARING FOR
YOUR PLANTS

Suppose you had planted your garden in soil. It would not have required your attention for a week or more: no growth would be seen before the plants took root. You would have watered it just after you put the seeds in the ground. There would be enough moisture in the soil to start the plants off. After that you might count on rain unless there was a dry spell and the garden needed watering. Even weeds would not crop up that soon. Unless your garden attracted hungry rabbits—and there is not much you could do about that except to fence it in—you would depend on nature for the start.

But your hydroponic garden requires care from the very moment you set the plants into the aggregate. The beds have been flooded with nutrient solution. So the roots are briefly immersed. Because they need oxygen (some is dissolved in the nutrients) you have to get air to them. This means almost immediate draining of the solution. If it took ten minutes to fill the bed within 1 inch (2.5 cm) of the gravel surface, then drainage should be accomplished within no more than twenty minutes. By the time drainage starts, the plants at the upper end of the bed are beginning to be aerated.

YOUR DAILY SCHEDULE

Some hours after the initial flooding you need to repeat the process and drain off the solution. The usual feeding schedule is twice a day. On very bright, hot days, growth and evaporation are greater than on cool, dull days. Then it may be necessary to feed three or even four times a day. To check whether you need to increase the frequency of watering, test the wetness or dryness of the aggregate. Just stick your finger down into it. This is a good rule to follow also in watering indoor plants potted in soil.

If the gravel is just moist about 1 inch (2.5 cm) from the surface, then stay with your two-a-day feeding. Don't ever forget that hydroponic growth is under *your* control. You cannot neglect your schedule if you want a good crop. Always be wary of overirrigation. Prevent water logging, which drowns the plants by "suffocation."

One other thing to remember: never feed at night. Photosynthesis stops in the absence of light. During the day the leaves give off oxygen as they produce sugar. At night, both roots and leaves utilize oxygen during their metabolism and give off carbon dioxide. If the roots are soaked, they are not getting oxygen and their metabolism is interferred with. *So never feed them at night.*

TESTING THE pH

While most crops tolerate a relatively wide range of pH—between pH 6.0 and 7.0—it is safer to have the pH at 6.5, still acid. There are several ways of testing the pH of the nutrient solution. If you are familiar with litmus paper you know that it changes color: red in acid, blue in alkaline, and it is purple in a neutral solution. However, since the pigment in litmus has a range of pH 4.5 to 8.3, it is not sufficiently sensitive to be useful for testing a hydroponic solution. For example, in a pH range of 6 to 7.5 it would very likely be purple, or neutral, at both pH 6+ and 7.5.

There is Nitrazine tape, obtainable in drug stores, which comes in a kit. The tape is dipped into a sample of nutrient solution. The color change is matched with a color scale in the kit that indicates the pH. Another kit furnishes a chemical that is dropped into a sample of nutrient solution. The chemical is called the *indicator.* One indicator is *brom thymol blue;* it is blue in alkali and yellow in acid.

The pH should be tested twice a week without fail. If the test shows the solution is alkaline, acid has to be added to lower the pH. Muriatic, sulfuric, or phosphoric acid may be used. However, the first two are very strong and must be used with great care to avoid getting on the skin or inhaling the vapor. A stock solution of 1 ounce (28 ml) of these acids added to 1 gallon (4.5 liters) of water is recommended. To raise the pH, a stock solution of 2 ounces (57 ml) of sodium or potassium hydroxide to 1 gallon (4.5 liters) of water, provides the right concentration to be added to reduce the acidity.

NUTRIENT
SOLUTION

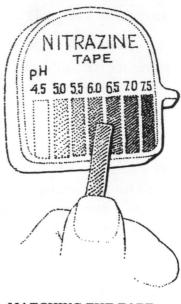

MATCHING THE TAPE
TO THE COLOR SCALE

NUTRIENT STRENGTH

As the plants grow they use up some of the nutrients. At the
end of about a week, the nutrient solution may have only
about 90 percent of the original concentration. This means
you have to make up the loss by adding nutrient. However,
it is more practical as well as more accurate to replace the
solution with freshly prepared formula. It is best to do this
regularly once a week.

If your supply tank is open, it should be covered with a
lid to reduce evaporation and prevent the growth of algae. If
at any time during the week the level of the solution is lower

than when first prepared, add enough water to bring it up to the original level.

WATCHING YOUR
GARDEN GROW

Taking care of a soilless garden requires no weeding and rarely spraying. If you follow the rules of maintaining your garden you need only observe the plants daily and enjoy seeing them grow. But observing means also being on the alert for signs of poor growth and of possible insect invasion.

Are the plants erect or bending to the side because of weak stems? Are the leaves small, pale, or wilted? It could be that they are not getting enough light. Or are the leaves scorched? Then they may be getting too much sunlight. Either way the garden may have to be relocated. This may be easy if it is a small indoor garden. In that case if the plants are getting too much sun, they should be moved. If they are not getting enough sunlight, overhead fluorescent lights or plant lights, special lamps that provide the ultra violet rays of the sun, will add to the amount of light.

Tomatoes, cucumbers, eggplant, and pole beans grow tall. In soil, tomatoes and pole beans have to be staked. At some point in their growth the stems will have to be supported. In a hydroponic garden this is done by stringing them up to an overhead wire. Circular clips that close like safety pins are placed around the base of the stem. Nylon vining cord is wound around the clip and hung on a hook on an overhead wire. Each plant grows like a vine and is kept erect as it grows.

IF TROUBLE COMES

When the plants are not thriving, several things may have gone wrong. The problem may be 1) improper care; 2) a nutrient deficiency has developed; 3) insects have invaded; 4) diseases, such as a fungus blight, or virus, has sickened the plants.

IMPROPER CARE

Let's say the leaves droop, turn yellow, and drop off. Check to see if the drainage pipe has become clogged, allowing the roots to sit wet. This could cause the leaves to look sickly. But leaves may also fall off when dry because of underwatering or excessive evaporation on very hot, dry days. Or has the nutrient solution not been changed when necessary? The solution may have become too concentrated by excessive evaporation, and the leaves have developed brown tips. Did you fail to add water to restore the proper level of the solution? If the leaves have turned black, it could be either from sun scald or sudden frost.

NUTRIENT DEFICIENCIES

If the plant seems to be slowed in its growth, and the leaves become a light green, almost yellow, it could be due to a nitrogen deficiency. Nitrogen, which the plant gets as nitrate, is as important to growth of plant tissues as protein is to animals! This deficiency may occur in very hot weather or during a period of rapid growth when the plant uses more nitrogen. In that case nitrogen must be added. The same symptoms may occur with insufficient phosphorus. Adding a third feeding daily of freshly prepared solution may be all that is necessary.

If there is a lack of potassium, the sodium-potassium balance is upset, and the leaves develop a sodium burn, recognized by brown coloration around the edges. It could also be due to a high sodium content in the water supply, so that the roots are taking up too much of this element. Too much sodium also interferes with the taking up of iron.

With iron deficiency, particularly in young plants, the leaves turn yellow, a condition called *chlorosis*. Iron uptake is also reduced by a high concentration of calcium in the solution, making it somewhat alkaline. And absorption of iron requires a low *p*H.

A magnesium deficiency causes the leaves to curl and is corrected by adding Epsom salts, or magnesium sulfate. A molybdenum deficiency shows up as leaf mottling; manganese lack delays blooming. Experienced growers get to recognize signs of imbalances and deficiencies and know when more magnesium, calcium, or iron is required, and they adjust the formula accordingly. It would be difficult to add molybdenum, one of the trace elements required in infinitesimally small quantities, so it would take a pharmacist's scale to weigh out the chemical—molybdenum trioxide. It is easier to add iron, which comes by the trade name Sequestrene, a green leaf stimulant, in which the iron is chemically bound. The chemical form is called 330 Fe iron chelate.

These minerals are available in garden supply stores and are sold individually, with instructions as to the quantity to dissolve in 1 gallon (4.5 liters) of solution. Sometimes the problem can be solved in another way. For instance, a greenhouse owner, who added Epsom salts to correct the deficiency of magnesium, found that when he changed to another supplier for his nutrient formula, he had no further deficiency problems. This shows that plants, like animals, vary, if ever so slightly, in their individual needs. It also explains why growers develop certain preferences based on their experience and why experimentation with formulas continues.

WHEN INSECTS MOVE IN

If insects are the problem you are likely to see it easily. Where do insect pests come from in a hydroponic garden? If your garden is outdoors close to other plants, that would be one way the insects reach it. Insect pests sometimes are on the underside of the leaf, but most of the time you will see them crawling on the upper surface and on the stem and fruit.

Aphids, or plant lice, are soft-bodied insects about a fifth of an inch (0.5 cm) long. With needle-sharp darts in their beaks, they pierce the stems and leaves. They are also found

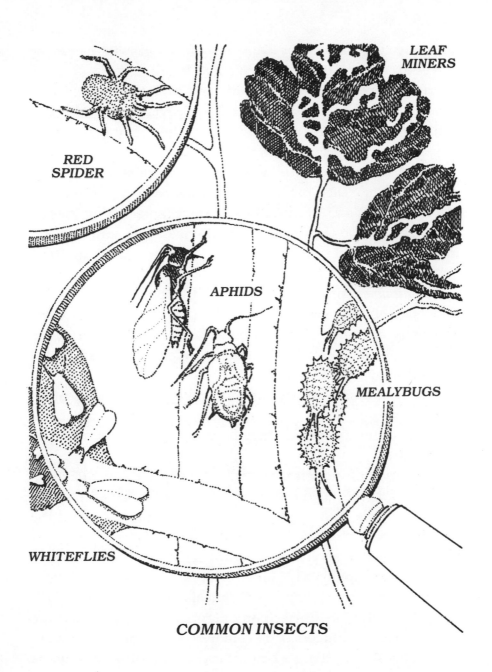

RED
SPIDER

LEAF
MINERS

APHIDS

MEALYBUGS

WHITEFLIES

COMMON INSECTS

around young roots. They stunt the plant's growth, cause the leaves to curl, and delay flowering and fruiting.

Leaf miners are the larvae of certain moths, flies, or sawflies. They feed on the surface cells of leaves, causing blisters and blotches. You will recognize them when they first appear as very tiny, white streaks on the leaves.

Red spiders are mites, not insects, but related to spiders and ticks. They suck the sap from leaves or young stems, discolor, weaken, and eventually kill the plants. Many species spin fine webs on the underside of the leaf. The spray recommended for these pests is *Kelthane,* two to four drops to 1 gallon (4.5 liters) of water.

Whiteflies, tiny insects related to aphids, feed on the underside of the leaves, causing the plant to wilt. They are especially abundant in warm climates and are the principal pests in greenhouses and plants kept indoors. They are killed with oil sprays and *Cygon,* an insecticide.

Mealybugs are among the most damaging of insect pests. The females of the species are wingless and crawl over the leaves and stems on which they feed. The plant wilts and ultimately dies.

If insect infestation is recognized early and insecticide repeatedly sprayed as necessary, the plant can be saved. Insecticides are available in feed stores, and it is wise to consult the supplier about the best one for the particular problem. For example, mealybugs can be killed with nicotine-sulfate sprays, whiteflies and aphids with Malathion.

Insecticides are poisonous chemicals and should be avoided for indoor gardens. Where many plants in a large garden are infested, either outdoors or in commercial greenhouses, spraying is almost the only way to attack the problem. For home use there are other remedies, if applied early and persistently.

Since the insects settle on the leaves, they can be washed off with soap and water, using a sudsy solution of ordinary laundry soap. *Be sure not to use detergent.* Apply your soap solution with cotton swabs, soaked in generous amounts. Insect eggs may not be so easy to remove by this method but can be dislodged by spraying the leaves with water. The insects can be picked off with cotton swabs dipped in alcohol or brushed off with a toothbrush.

If you follow the rule of *daily observation,* you will detect the insect problem early and are likely to rid your plants of these pests. You may well have to repeat the applications; persistence is essential.

PLANTS HAVE
DISEASES TOO

Tobacco leaves get *tobacco mosaic,* a disease caused by viruses. Grain crops have *blights* and *rusts,* which are fungal diseases. And hydroponic tomatoes, even in well-kept greenhouses, may be attacked by a virus which may be the same or similar to the tobacco leaf mosaic virus. Fungal disease is likely to occur when there is a high buildup of humidity. Such a condition favors leaf mold, called *Cladosporium fulvum* and gray mold (*Botrytis cinerea*). Both are treated with a chemical—Orthocide 50, a garden fungicide (50 stands for 50% Captan)—or with Captan, a general disinfectant useful for washing down the walls of the greenhouse. This is equally good for curing plants of fungal disease. One grower recommends dissolving 8 teaspoons (40 ml) of Captan in 1 gallon (4.5 liters) of water, and spraying it on the plants.

VISIT TO A
COMMERCIAL
GREENHOUSE

Is there a commercial hydroponic greenhouse in your neighborhood or within easy reach in another town? If you can make arrangements in advance for a visit, you will be able to see plants grown in a controlled environment, with fully automated operations. You are likely to find owners proud of their flourishing soilless gardens. They will be glad to explain how a sophisticated hydroponic unit works and how to get a good yield of a healthy crop in a year-round food factory.

Such a hydroponic unit is usually housed in what is known as a quonset type building, a semicylindrical structure. Can you imagine a 150-foot (46-m) cylinder, 12 feet (3.7 m) in diameter, cut in half, and set on the ground. The nearest thing to it in shape is an airplane hangar. The roof and sides are one, called the *cover*. It rests on a concrete floor. The cover is made of polyvinyl chloride (PVC) plastic sheeting or corrugated fiberglass. Both materials are semiclear to let in sunlight, yet durable and strong enough to resist wind, withstand pelting rain, and keep out the cold. Where extremes of temperature are a problem, the cover is made of two layers with an air space between to provide insulation. During the summer heat, in places like Arizona or southern Florida, some shade is necessary. In one greenhouse this was achieved with sheets of butcher paper strung across the upper part of the cover.

However complicated the structure inside may appear, every hydroponic unit still has the same three essential parts: container, aggregate, and water supply. Completely enclosed, the plants grow safely away from the "elements"—rain, frost, heat, and seasonal changes.

In one Floridian greenhouse the *container* consists of four or five concrete vats or beds set in parallel rows, alternating with concrete walks. The beds are 110 feet (about 34 m) long, 2 feet (0.6 m) wide, and sunken to a depth of 8 inches (20 cm). The *aggregate* is gravel. When filled, the beds are about level with the walkways.

At the time of our visit to this particular greenhouse the beds were planted with tomatoes. (If one wanted to grow lettuce, low growing plants, they would be set in fiberglass trays arranged one above the other like shelves. This is done to utilize the overhead space. Saving space is an important feature of hydroponic gardening.)

Running the full length on the floor of each bed is a PVC pipe, 3 inches (7.5 cm) in diameter. It is perforated at 6-inch (15-cm) intervals with four holes around its circumference. As the roots grow they reach into these openings in the pipe, coming in contact with the nutrient solution. The aggregate in this system serves only for support of the roots.

The *water source* is a well, about 20 feet (about 6 m) from the greenhouse. Water is pumped in through a plastic pipe directly into the sump tank in the greenhouse. The sump tank contains the nutrient solution. It is located under the floor, at a level about 2 feet (0.6 m) below the gravel beds. Inside it a pump sends the nutrient solution through the PVC pipe at the bottom of the gravel beds.

Here we see the first automated control mechanism. The sump pump is activated by a timer, an electric clock set for cyclical flooding two or more times a day, as needed. In this operation it takes 15 minutes for the pump to flood the beds. The pump automatically stops flooding, and the pipe is drained by gravity into the sump tank. In addition, there is a slope of 2 inches (5 cm) in the beds that assists in gravity drainage.

CONTROL OF THE ENVIRONMENT

The most important automatic operations are those that maintain a nearly constant environment. The air is heated or cooled and circulated, and its humidity adjusted to desired levels. A heater, controlled by thermostat, goes on at night or other times when the temperature falls and goes off at the temperature for which it is set. A system of fans circulates and distributes filtered air evenly through the greenhouse. A cooling system, which also humidifies the air, is located at the back wall. The wall is open or closed by means of swinging louvers that act like vents; they are operated by several small motors. The upper part of the wall is faced on the outside by pads of excelsior or aspen chips spread between layers of wire

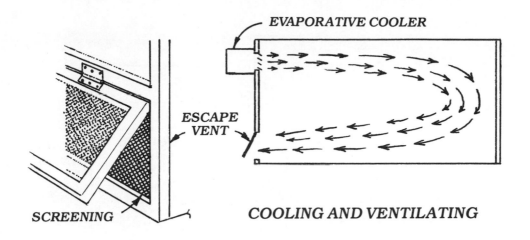

EVAPORATIVE COOLER

ESCAPE
VENT

SCREENING

COOLING AND VENTILATING

called *hardware cloth*. The pads are misted by an outside water spray. Cool, moist air flows in through the opened louvers when the motors go on.

Together these mechanisms provide the proper temperature. For tomato plants this is 75° to 80° F (24° to 27° C) on sunny days and about ten degrees lower on cloudy days; 60° to 65° F (15° to 18° C) at night.

When the temperature drops to below 60° F (15° C), the heater, controlled by a thermostat, goes on and protects the plants even against frost.

STARTING THE PLANTS

In large operations such as this one, the plants are not started in soil but in *sterile* seed containers: Jiffy Pellets, cubes, or GRO-blocks. Mainly this is done to avoid introducing soil organisms, but it also saves time and space. Two seeds are

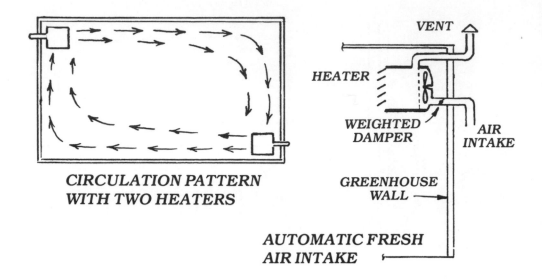

**CIRCULATION PATTERN
WITH TWO HEATERS**

VENT

HEATER

WEIGHTED
DAMPER

AIR
INTAKE

GREENHOUSE
WALL

**AUTOMATIC FRESH
AIR INTAKE**

placed on each seed container, which expands when dampened with water. In the pressure of moisture the seeds germinate, and the plant breaks through with true leaves (sometimes only one seed germinates). When both seeds germinate and one plant is taller and about 3 inches (7.5 cm) high, the shorter one is pulled out. The taller one, *still sitting in the seed starting container,* is placed right into the aggregate.

ROUTINE CARE

From then on the plants are cared for in the same way as in a homegrown garden, except that feeding and draining are automatically controlled. The *p*H of the nutrient solution is tested twice a week, the sump tank level checked and restored, the nutrient solution replaced weekly or less frequently as demanded by rate of growth. Daily observation of the plants is important even in a controlled setting. It is the best assurance of a healthy crop. The grower checks the rate of growth, leaf proliferation (spread), curling, puckering, paling, or mottling of the leaves. The grower is also on the alert for the appearance of insects or signs of disease and decides what is to be done to cope with any such problems. This kind of care is not automatically controlled but requires the personal and expert attention of the grower.

UPRIGHT SUPPORT

When the plants reach a height of 4 or 5 feet (1.2 or 1.5 m) they need to have support. A plastic clip like a circular safety pin is placed around the bottom of the stem. Nylon cord is attached to the clip and the other end looped over a hook attached to an overhead wire.

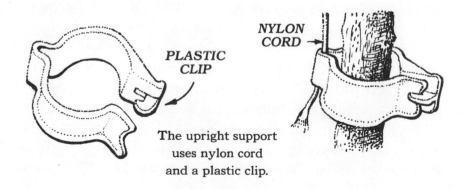

PLASTIC CLIP

NYLON CORD →

The upright support uses nylon cord and a plastic clip.

POLLINATION

A greenhouse tomato grower has one other daily chore, which the farmer raising tomatoes in soil does not have to be concerned about, or would find it impractical. That chore is pollinating the flower clusters. (The tomato plant is self-pollinated—its flowers have both the male and female parts.) Grown outdoors, the transfer of pollen from the stamen to the pistil is helped by wind. To increase pollination the greenhouse grower uses a little vibrating gadget or an electric razor directed to the stem. The vibration of the razor helps shed the pollen free as a fine yellow dust. Once pollinated, the blossom begins to form into the fruit.

SANITATION

It has been said that no part of care of a hydroponic system is more important than sanitation in and around the greenhouse. The very enclosure of the plants helps to protect them from diseases, insects, and other predators. The walkways are kept clean inside, and weeds around the outside of the building are kept down because they invite insect pests and diseases. Visitors are asked to brush their shoes on a chemically-treated cleansing mat at the entrance. And would it surprise you to find a NO SMOKING sign over the door? For reasons of smoke pollution? No, but tobacco in any form in the greenhouse carries the risk of tomato mosaic virus, a plant disease most difficult to control. Prevention of infestation and disease is better than having to cure with pesticides. That is the golden rule for soilless gardening.

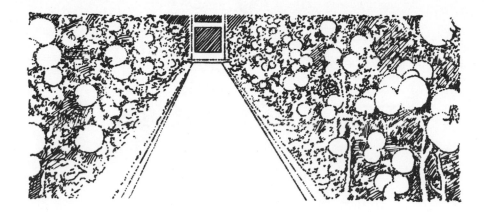

REAPING THE HARVEST

The number of crops a year depends on climate and on the plant selected, since some vegetables ripen more quickly than others. If sunshine and warm days may be counted on almost the year round, as in southern Florida and parts of California, at least two crops of tomatoes may be harvested and three to four of cucumbers. The fruit should be picked as soon as it is ripe. If allowed to remain on the vine, especially during hot days, the fruit may have cracks.

When picked, hydroponic tomatoes are red, firm, and thin-skinned. Tomatoes bought in supermarkets have been picked before ripening, often sprayed with ethylene gas, and may not get to your table until a month after picking.

If you happen to visit the hydroponic greenhouse at the height of fruiting, you will find the plants weighted down with luscious fruit. In the same growing space the yield by weight of marketable hydroponic tomatoes is ten or more times that of soil-grown tomatoes.

RESEARCH GOES ON

Hydroponic culture is established as a practical method of growing a wide variety of vegetables, berries, and some grain crops. But studies continue to research the conditions in which each species will grow best. With this purpose in mind the Agricultural Research Service of the United States Department of Agriculture in Fargo, North Dakota, is experimenting with a long list of crops, among them endive, carrot, corn, okra, soybean, sugarcane, and turnip. For example, peas grow best in cool temperatures and short days, while barley requires higher temperatures and longer days. If they are grown side by side the year round, neither will reach its maximum level of growth. These experiments determined the best conditions of temperature, light, length of day, and time to reach maturity for each of over fifty crops.

Here is a sample of what they found as shown in a table from their report.

PLANT	LENGTH OF DAYLIGHT (HRS.)	TEMPERATURE °C (DAY–NIGHT)	MATURITY (DAYS)
Pea	12	20–15	60
Melon	14	30–23	60
Squash	14	30–23	60
Potato	12	21–16	75
Tomato	14	25–25	100

Conclusion: Peas and melons do not have the same requirements for optimal growth, but melons and squash do grow best under the same conditions. So melons and squash could be paired for the best results, while potatoes and tomatoes grown under the same conditions would yield only average results.

Other experiments with the right seeding depth, germination requirements, optimal nutrient needs, and harvesting periods for each species yield information for crop improvement.

Also being investigated are types of containers, different growing media, and different methods of watering. Is spraying roots from below or the spreading of nutrients dry and watering from above the better system? How best can the kinds and amount of nutrients to the plants be regulated? How can new varieties of vegetables with desired properties be produced? For instance, we are told that for people who have digestive difficulties with tomatoes and cucumbers, it is now possible to produce a low-acid tomato and a "no-burp" cucumber. Tomatoes with extra calcium for babies and more iron for invalids have been reported. An odorless, "no-weep" onion is perhaps to come! There is a healthy skepticism as to whether such qualities are the result of hydroponic culture techniques or rather the result of genetic or breeding methods. But laboratory experiments do go on.

Commercial growers want to know not only which crops can be grown at the same time in the same beds under the same conditions. They are also concerned about cost and marketability of hydroponic crops compared with soil-grown crops.

A vegetable specialist and an economist at the University of California, Riverside, tackled that problem in a survey of the hydroponic industry in California. In their report, "Sample Costs for Producing Tomatoes and Cucumbers in California," they gave complete and detailed information on greenhouse structures, labor, equipment, and other costs, such as depreciation of the growing structure, its useful life (in years), of grading and packing, taxes and insurance.

They found that the fuel, power, and labor added to the high cost of constructing a properly designed and equipped greenhouse structure made the operation of soilless culture costly. For the same amount of growing space, the labor, material, and equipment of *soil* bed culture, including the cost of tillage and raking to preharvest, was well below that of a hydroponic operation. However, hydroponics had advantages that counterbalanced the lower cost of soil farming: two or three harvest periods, larger and better quality fruit, and a much higher estimated annual yield per 1,000 square feet (about 100 sq m) of greenhouse space.

Still, what is the cost per pound (0.45 kg) to you the consumer? Let's say that in the same season in the same area you may pay forty-five cents for a pound (0.45 kg) of soil-grown tomatoes and eighty-five cents for a pound (0.45 kg) of hydroponic tomatoes. Which you buy will depend on how you value the difference in quality as against the difference in cost. Hydroponic growers say that their products cannot compete with soil-grown products. This may well explain the relatively small number of commercial growers, as the survey of the industry in California revealed.

This survey proved valuable to both prospective growers and those already operating. But the information is of little concern to the hydroponicist who gets tastier and healthier vegetables on the plate, while experiencing the joy of growing a crop for use.

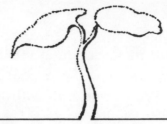

SCORE CARD FOR SOILLESS GARDENING

To what extent does hydroponics fill a need for more and better food? Let's see how this pioneering branch of horticulture is scored today.

WHAT ARE
THE ADVANTAGES?

Imagine crops grown on coral islands where no soil exists; or in places where the soil is infertile or contaminated with disease; or where the drainage is poor or water is scarce.

Excellent yields are possible in a fraction of the space required by soil-grown crops. And so much of land space is too expensive for soil farming.

Without the need for tilling, cultivating, manuring and weeding, much of the labor of soil farming is avoided.

Hydroponics is a way of conserving water; only a small proportion of the water required in soil culture is used. As much or more than 90 percent of water is saved.

Pollution of land and streams by chemical fertilizers and pesticides in runoff from fields is not a problem.

With proper care there is less tendency for crops to develop diseases.

Balanced nutrient feeding and regular irrigation in a controlled environment of an automated greenhouse produces a uniformly healthier crop. There is no need to pick out bad fruit and select for grading.

The plants are vine-ripened, attractive in appearance, superior in flavor, and don't spoil as quickly as field tomatoes.

It is even possible, by increasing the nitrogen level, to regulate the phases of growth, such as flowering and fruiting for taller plants, fleshier fruit with fewer seeds.

AGRONOMISTS POINT TO DISADVANTAGES

While soilless crops are generally free of diseases, when they do become infected the condition spreads rapidly to the whole crop through the recycling of the nutrients. In soil, many microorganisms will kill the disease-causing organisms.

In the soil the nutrients and natural fertilizers are released slowly but steadily, depending on the rate of their withdrawal by the roots.

Since most of our vegetables have been developed and are adapted to growth in soil, the development of new crop varieties will require further research.

Root vegetables such as carrots, parsnips, beets, and tubers, such as potatoes, become misshapen by gravel and may need a special growing medium.

More important than these drawbacks is the factor of cost not only for the construction and the equipment for automated control but for the kind of labor required. The routine care of a hydroponic system requires trained personnel to manage the operation and to handle special problems. The workers need also to understand the requirements of plant growth and the principles of nutrition.

A balanced view of hydroponics also requires that its present limitations be examined.

LIMITS

The high cost of commercial hydroponic culture limits the market to the production of gourmet items for consumers who will pay high prices for high quality vegetables in and out of season. As a mass production industry, hydroponics is not likely to be economically feasible.

What is the outlook for feeding a hungry world? Will it be a way to feed the millions of hungry and undernourished millions in the developing countries? On the table of an average Indian family, four-fifths of the food is rice, some wheat, corn, peas, and soybeans. Grain is the staple of the diet of three-fourths of the people of the world. In such countries as India, Iran, Spain, Mexico, Brazil, Guatemala, Philippines, Samoa, and the Seychelles, soilless gardening is undoubtedly adding some variety to the drab and nutritionally deficient diet. But it cannot be looked on as a solution for the world's food problem.

WHERE HYDROPONICS
HAS A FUTURE

In nearly every corner of the globe homemakers, amateur gardeners, and hobbyists have discovered that soilless culture can be a rewarding activity. It can provide fresh food crops for the table and indoor flower gardens to beautify the home.

James Sholto Douglas, Consulting Member, International Working-Group on Soilless Culture writes: "No matter how small your soilless garden may be, even one or two pot plants or a few window boxes, you are still utilizing the technique of international science."

Hydroponics is especially suitable for people living in cities, even in apartments, for without soil and mess one can grow vegetables. Besides enriching the diet and improving nutrition, the soilless garden provides great satisfaction of creation and pleasure.

Hydroponics has also come to the schools. Its educational value in opening up a path to the study of plant biology and scientific techniques is being recognized. Thanks to innovative teachers, a hydroponic garden is increasingly becoming part of the science curriculum. What an exciting practical experience as a school science project!

Inevitably it should lead to more hydroponics enthusiasts and knowledgeable practitioners of the art.

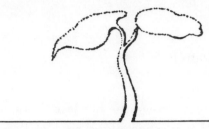

READING LIST

BOOKS

Bridwell, Raymond. *Hydroponic Gardening*. Santa Barbara, California: Woodbridge Press Publishing Company, 1974.

Dickerman, Alexandra and John. *Discovering Hydroponic Gardening*. Santa Barbara, California: Woodbridge Press Publishing Company, 1975.

Douglas, James Sholto. *Beginner's Guide to Hydroponics*. New York: Drake Publishers Inc., 1977.

Kramer, Jack. *Gardens Without Soil—House Plants, Vegetables & Flowers*. New York: Charles Scribner's Sons, 1976.

Sullivan, George. *Understanding Hydroponics*. New York: Warne, 1976.

BULLETINS

(Arranged alphabetically by state university)

"Hydroponics: A Guide to Soilless Culture Systems." Leaflet 2947, Feb. 1977. Division of Agricultural Sciences, University of California, Riverside 92502.

"Hydroponic Culture of Vegetable Crops," by M. E. Marvel, Institute of Food and Agriculture Sciences, University of Florida, Gainesville, Fl. 32611.

"Vegetable Gardening in Florida," by James S. Stephens, 1976. Institute of Food and Agricultural Sciences, University of Florida, Gainesville, Fl. 32611.

"Nutriculture System. Growing Plants Without Soil." Station Bulletin No. 44, March 1974. Department of Horticulture Agricultural Experiment Station, Purdue University, West Lafayette, Indiana 47907.

"Growing Plants with Nutrient Solutions without Soil." New Jersey Leaflet 423. Cooperative Extension Service, Rutgers, The State University of New Jersey, New Brunswick, N.J. 08901.

"Growing Ornamental Greenhouse Crops in Gravel Culture." Special Circular 92, 1956. Ohio Agricultural Experiment Station, The Ohio State University, Wooster, Ohio 44691.

"Gravel Culture for Growing Ornamental Greenhouse Crops." Research Bulletin 679, 1948. Ohio Agricultural Experiment Station, The Ohio State University, Wooster, Ohio 44691.

If *your* state university has an Agricultural Experiment Station or Department of Agriculture or Horticulture, write for information on gardening without soil.

SELECTED LIST OF SUPPLIERS

Aqua-Gro, Inc.
Box 827
Powell, Wyoming 82435

Bruce & Mallow Distributing Co.
Route 2, Box 201 B
Cumberland, Maryland 21502

Casey Hydroponic
Box 1121
Wilkes-Barre, Pennsylvania 18701

Consolidated Laboratories, Inc.
910 S. Hohokam Drive, Suite 118
Tempe, Arizona 85281

Continental Nutriculture
Box 6751
Lubbock, Texas 79413

Dr. Chatalier's Plant Food Co.
Box 20375
St. Petersburg, Florida 33742

Eckroat Seed Co.
1106 N. Eastern Ave.
Oklahoma City, Oklahoma 73117

Florida Grow Box
3004 Kelvington Drive
Orlando, Florida 32810

Food for Everyone
3000 Cienega
Hollister, California 95023

Gro-Master Hydroponics
McKee Road, Box E
Collegedale, Tennessee 37315

Hill, Ray D.
P.O. Box 1243
Cocoa Beach, Florida 32931

Hydro-Gardens of Denver
3900 Magnolia Unit A
Denver, Colorado 80207

Hydro-Growth Greenhouses, Inc.
21675 W. Doral Road
Brookfield Township
Waukesha, Wisconsin 53186

Hydroponic Chemical Company
Copley, Ohio 44321

The Hydroponics Company
Box 3215
Little Rock, Arkansas 72203

Hydroponics Industries, Inc.
95 Grande Boulevard
Denver, Colorado 80223

Hydroponics of Nevada, Inc.
808 S. Decatur
Las Vegas, Nevada 89107

Mellinger's Inc.
2310 W. South Range
North Lima, Ohio 44452

Modular Hydroponic Gardens
P.O. Box 8121
Fountain Valley, California 92708

Pacific Aquaculture
3 A Gate 5 Road
Sausalito, California 94965

South Bay Grow Box
2047 Lomita Boulevard
Lomita, California 90707

Sterling Service Co.
249 Thompson Drive
Dalton, Georgia 30720

Water Garden
1332 E. Katella
Anaheim, California 92805

Before you write to any of the above companies for supplies, check with your local nursery center, lawn and garden center, hardware and feed stores, and plant nurseries.

The International Working-Group on Soilless Culture (IWOSC) is based in Wageningen, The Netherlands. Volunteer representatives in many parts of the world may be consulted.

Consultants in:

E. Head
P.O. Box 386
Estancia, New Mexico 87016

THE UNITED STATES

A. Pilgrim
Hydroculture Inc.
1516 North 7th Avenue
Phoenix, Arizona 85007

T. C. Broyer
Department of Plant Nutrition
3044 Life Science Building
Berkeley, California 94704

J. L. Weihing
Department of Plant Pathology
University of Nebraska
    East Campus
Lincoln, Nebraska 68503

J. K. Choate
Pan American Hydroponics Inc.
P.O. Box 470
Grapevine, Texas 76051

J. J. Hanan
Department of Horticulture
Fort Collins, Colorado 80521

F. M. Yamaguchi
12727 Saratoga Creek Drive
Saratoga, California 95070

GREAT BRITAIN

CANADA

E. J. Hewitt
Horticultural Research Station
Long Ashton, Bristol
England

R. M. Adamson
Research Station
Canadian Department
    of Agriculture
Saanichton, British Columbia
Canada

J. W. S. Richmond
Whitehall Nursery
Whitehall Road
Peel, near Blackpool
England

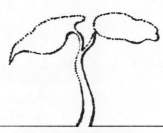

INDEX